ENDANGERED AND THREATENED ANIMALS

THE GOPHER TORTOISE

A MyReportLinks.com Book

Donald G. Schueler

MyReportLinks.com Books

an imprint of

Enslow Publishers, Inc. **E**

Box 398, 40 Industrial Road
Berkeley Heights, NJ 07922
USA

MyReportLinks.com Books, an imprint of Enslow Publishers, Inc. MyReportLinks is a trademark of Enslow Publishers, Inc.

Library of Congress Cataloging-in-Publication Data

Schueler, Donald G.
  The gopher tortoise / Donald G. Schueler.
    p. cm. — (Endangered and threatened animals)
Summary: Discusses what gopher tortoises are, why they are endangered, what their current status is, and what is being done to help them. Includes Internet links to Web sites related to gopher tortoises. Includes bibliographical references (p.   ).
  ISBN 0-7660-5053-X
  1. Gopher tortoise—Juvenile literature. 2. Endangered species—Juvenile literature. [1. Gopher tortoise. 2. Turtles. 3. Endangered species.] I. Title. II. Series.
  QL666.C584 S38 2003
  597.92—dc21
                                            2002008997

Printed in the United States of America

10 9 8 7 6 5 4 3 2 1

To Our Readers:
Through the purchase of this book, you and your library gain access to the Report Links that specifically back up this book.

The Publisher will provide access to the Report Links that back up this book and will keep these Report Links up to date on **www.myreportlinks.com** for three years from the book's first publication date.

We have done our best to make sure all Internet addresses in this book were active and appropriate when we went to press. However, the author and the Publisher have no control over, and assume no liability for, the material available on those Internet sites or on other Web sites they may link to.

The usage of the MyReportLinks.com Books Web site is subject to the terms and conditions stated on the Usage Policy Statement on **www.myreportlinks.com**.

In the future, a password may be required to access the Report Links that back up this book. The password is found on the bottom of page 4 of this book.

Any comments or suggestions can be sent by e-mail to comments@myreportlinks.com or to the address on the back cover.

Photo Credits: © Corel Corporation, p. 3; California Turtle & Tortoise Club, p. 30; Courtesy of MyReportLinks.com Books, p. 4; Desert Tortoise Preserve Committee, p. 25; Desertusa.com, p. 35; Enchanted Forest Nature Sanctuary, pp. 12, 33, 38; Fort Matanzas National Monument, p. 20; Georgia State Parks and Historic Sites, p. 41; John Bavaro, p. 14; Kennedy Space Center, p. 19; Photo by Brian D. Enslow, p. 43; Photo by Charles Bush, p. 1; Photo by Thomas Warhol, pp. 23, 28; Photographer, Michael J. Conner, p. 36; The Wild Ones Animal Index, p. 15; Tortoise Group, p. 39; United States Fish and Wildlife Service, p. 45; University of Florida, pp. 17, 26.

Cover Photo: Photo by Charles Bush

Contents

MyReportLinks.com Books
Great Books, Great Links, Great for Research!

MyReportLinks.com Books present the information you need to learn about your report subject. In addition, they show you where to go on the Internet for more information. The pre-evaluated Report Links that back up this book are kept up to date on **www.myreportlinks.com**. With the purchase of a MyReportLinks.com Books title, you and your library gain access to the Report Links that specifically back up that book. The Report Links save hours of research time and link to dozens—even hundreds—of Web sites, source documents, and photos related to your report topic.

Please see "To Our Readers" on the Copyright page for important information about this book, the MyReportLinks.com Books Web site, and the Report Links that back up this book.

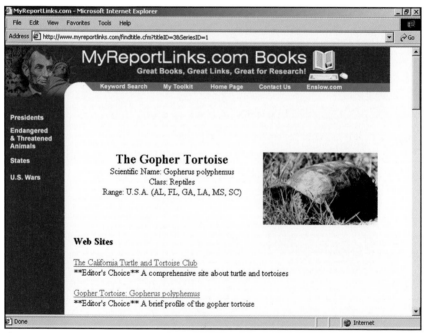

Access:

The Publisher will provide access to the Report Links that back up this book and will try to keep these Report Links up to date on our Web site for three years from the book's first publication date. Please enter **EGT1989** if asked for a password.

Report Links

The Internet sites described below can be accessed at
http://www.myreportlinks.com

▶ **The California Turtle and Tortoise Club**   *EDITOR'S CHOICE
The California Turtle and Tortoise Club helps preserve turtles and
tortoises worldwide. There is good information on many species,
including diet, range, and threats. You can even listen to the voices of
six kinds of tortoises!

Link to this Internet site from http://www.myreportlinks.com
*EDITOR'S CHOICE

▶ **Gopher Tortoise: Gopherus polyphemus**
At this Web site you will find a brief profile of the gopher tortoise.
Here you will learn about its physical characteristics, endangered status,
breeding, habitat, and range.

Link to this Internet site from http://www.myreportlinks.com
*EDITOR'S CHOICE

▶ **National Wildlife Federation**
National Wildlife Federation's goal is to raise awareness and involve the
public in protecting the environment. Their information on the desert
tortoise is comprehensive. Searching the site brings up even more
articles on tortoises.

Link to this Internet site from http://www.myreportlinks.com
*EDITOR'S CHOICE

▶ **Gopherus polyphemus**
This site confirms the tortoise's reputation as a slow mover, reporting
that the average pace of a Florida gopher tortoise is less than half a mile
per hour. There is plenty of other interesting information as well.

Link to this Internet site from http://www.myreportlinks.com
*EDITOR'S CHOICE

▶ **Endangered Species**
At this Web site you will find links to the endangered species list,
extinct species, species facts and data, and other useful information. You
will also find links to endangered species organizations around the
world.

Link to this Internet site from http://www.myreportlinks.com
*EDITOR'S CHOICE

▶ **Gopher Tortoise Council**
At the Gopher Tortoise Council Web site, you will learn about efforts
being made to protect the gopher tortoise. You will also find facts about
the gopher tortoise's history, habitat, legal status, and much more.

Link to this Internet site from http://www.myreportlinks.com

 The Internet sites described below can be accessed at
http://www.myreportlinks.com

▶**Amphibians and Reptiles of Fort Matanzas National Monument**
The gopher tortoise is one of the most abundant reptile species at Fort
Matanzas National Monument in Florida. This site provides very good
information on their burrows, their "roommates," and their diet.

Link to this Internet site from http://www.myreportlinks.com

▶**Desert Animal Survival**
Desert USA offers some interesting information about how animals survive
the desert's harsh environment. Learn how desert-dwelling species have
adapted to a life with little water and very high temperatures.

Link to this Internet site from http://www.myreportlinks.com

▶**The Desert Tortoise**
Whether you are looking for a quick reference on the Desert Tortoise or more
extensive information, this site has what you need. The basic facts are laid
out in table form at the top of the page, followed by a lengthy profile with all
the details.

Link to this Internet site from http://www.myreportlinks.com

▶**The Desert Tortoise Recovery Plan**
This paper, presented at an international conference on tortoise conservation,
spells out a federal recovery plan for the desert tortoise population in part of
its range, where it is listed as a threatened species.

Link to this Internet site from http://www.myreportlinks.com

▶**Desert Tortoise Natural Area Virtual Field Trip**
Take a virtual tour of the Desert Tortoise Natural Area in California. This
site has beautiful photos of a refuge created by the Desert Tortoise Preserve
Committee. Useful links tell about the preserves other wildlife.

Link to this Internet site from http://www.myreportlinks.com

▶**The Endangered Species Program**
At the U.S. Fish & Wildlife Service Web site you will find many resources
about endangered species, including legislation, species information, a kids'
page, and much more.

Link to this Internet site from http://www.myreportlinks.com

The Internet sites described below can be accessed at
http://www.myreportlinks.com

▶ **Fire Ecology and Management**
Fire is necessary for preserving suitable habitat for many species,
including the gopher tortoise. The Kennedy Space Center's site
offers detailed gopher tortoise species and habitat information.

Link to this Internet site from http://www.myreportlinks.com

▶ **Gopher Tortoises**
This site, maintained by a Florida nature sanctuary, offers detailed
information about the life and behavior of the gopher tortoise. It is
richly illustrated with photographs of tortoise habitat.

Link to this Internet site from http://www.myreportlinks.com

▶ **Gopher Tortoises**
This site offers a quick-reference fact sheet on the gopher tortoise.
Although some of the specific regulations apply only to Florida, most
of the information applies to the tortoise in all of its range.

Link to this Internet site from http://www.myreportlinks.com

▶ **Gopher Tortoise**
The Florida Fish and Wildlife Conservation Commission offers a brief
profile of the gopher tortoise. Here you will learn why the status of the
gopher tortoise in Florida is of concern.

Link to this Internet site from http://www.myreportlinks.com

▶ **Gopher Tortoise—David Rostal**
At this PBS Web site you will learn about some of the challenges in
studying the gopher tortoise from David Rostal. You will also learn
about some discoveries made through the "Burrow Cam."

Link to this Internet site from http://www.myreportlinks.com

▶ **Gopher Tortoise Fact Sheet**
This Web site provides facts about the gopher tortoise. Here you will
learn about its habitat, range, breeding, feeding, survival, threats, and
other facts.

Link to this Internet site from http://www.myreportlinks.com

The Internet sites described below can be accessed at
http://www.myreportlinks.com

▶**Gopher Tortoise, Gopherus polyphemus**
This Web site provides a brief profile of the gopher tortoise. Here you will
learn about its classification, physical characteristics, life cycle, history, range,
and conservation status.

Link to this Internet site from http://www.myreportlinks.com

▶**The Gopher Tortoise: A Species in Decline**
The University of Florida's Web site offers a realistic report on the gopher
tortoise's outlook in that state. Some of the projections are out of date,
but there is still good information on the tortoises' role as a keystone
species in Florida.

Link to this Internet site from http://www.myreportlinks.com

▶**The Law and the Tortoise**
There are many regulations in place to help protect desert tortoises in
Nevada from collectors and builders. This site explains the regulations and
tells why sometimes even helping a tortoise cross a busy road can be
dangerous for the animal.

Link to this Internet site from http://www.myreportlinks.com

▶**Live Freshwater Turtle and Tortoise Trade in the United States**
This Humane Society of the United States report tells of the dangers posed by
the worldwide trade in turtles and tortoises. Accounts of inhumane shipping
practices are horrifying. The report urges changes in existing laws.

Link to this Internet site from http://www.myreportlinks.com

▶**Mexican Bolson Tortoise (Gopherus flavomarginatus)**
The Mexican, or Bolson, tortoise was not identified as a distinct species until
1958. This Wildlife Trust site offers a brief account of the discovery of this
species and tells of efforts to preserve it.

Link to this Internet site from http://www.myreportlinks.com

▶*National Wildlife* **magazine**
The raven poses an increasing threat to the desert tortoise. Ravens are
responsible for fifty percent of juvenile desert tortoise deaths in some areas.

Link to this Internet site from http://www.myreportlinks.com

The Internet sites described below can be accessed at
http://www.myreportlinks.com

▶ **A Natural History of the Desert Tortoise**
Visit this site to learn more about the life of the desert tortoise, which
inhabits the Mojave and Sonoran Deserts of the southwestern United
States as well as desert areas of nearby Mexico.

Link to this Internet site from http://www.myreportlinks.com

▶ **The New York Turtle and Tortoise Society**
NYTTS addresses the care and conservation of tortoises and turtles
worldwide. Search for gopher, desert, and Bolson tortoises to find
abstracts of scientific papers on topics like recovery plans, health, and
habitat studies.

Link to this Internet site from http://www.myreportlinks.com

▶ **Partners in Amphibian and Reptile Conservation**
On this teacher-friendly page you can access lots of great fact sheets on
animals that live in the southeastern United States. The sheets on the
gopher tortoise and the Sandhills habitat are excellent research resources.

Link to this Internet site from http://www.myreportlinks.com

▶ **The Texas Tortoise**
From the Texas Parks and Wildlife Department comes this profile of
the Texas tortoise, closely related to gopher, Bolson, and desert
tortoises. It was listed as a threatened species in Texas in 1977 but is
not yet federally listed.

Link to this Internet site from http://www.myreportlinks.com

▶ **TortoiseAid's Burrow on the Net**
TortoiseAid International is dedicated "to the protection and
preservation of tortoises, turtles, and terrapins worldwide." Its site
provides excellent links to a wide range of information about tortoises,
particularly North American species.

Link to this Internet site from http://www.myreportlinks.com

▶ **Turtles and Tortoises**
At the World Almanac for Kids Online you will find basic
information about the physical characteristics, behavior, and types
of turtles and tortoises.

Link to this Internet site from http://www.myreportlinks.com

Gopher Tortoise Facts

Class
Reptilia

Family
Testudinidae

Genus
Gopherus

Species
Polyphemus

Status
Listed by United States
Fish and Wildlife Service
(USFWS) as a threatened
species on July 7, 1987.

Range
AL, FL, GA, LA, MS, SC

Gestation Period
80 to 100 days

Breeding Season
Usually Spring

Habitat
Forests (usually pine forests) and
grassy areas with well-drained
sandy soils

Shell Size
5.9 to 14.6 inches

Life Span
40 to 60 years

Weight
Up to 15 pounds

Home Territory
Approximately 8 acres

Threats to Survival
Habitat loss, URTD,
predators, cars

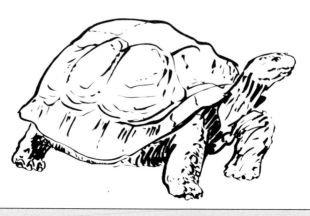

The Gopher in the Garden

When a neighbor told me a gopher was eating the lettuce in my garden, I thought he was kidding me. When he added that I should catch the gopher because it was good to eat, I decided he must be crazy. I knew that gophers were small rodents, about the size of a rat, and that they lived out West, not here in the Deep South. Still, even if they did live down here, who would want to eat one?

This was way back in 1968. I had just bought eighty acres of pine woodlands in southern Mississippi. I had planted a little vegetable garden. I did not take gardening very seriously, but I was curious to find out what was nipping away at my newly sprouted lettuce. That night, after my neighbor's visit, I went out to the garden with a flashlight. There I found my mystery salad eater—not a rodent, but a great big land turtle. As I would later learn, my neighbor had been right after all. I was indeed looking at a "gopher"—*Gopherus polyphemus*, the gopher tortoise!

I did not know a thing about gopher tortoises back then. However, I was thrilled to have this unexpected species of wildlife living on my property. The gopher, on the other hand, was not so thrilled to have me living on his property. He hurried toward a nearby hole in the ground. Earlier, I had noticed the hole, but I thought it had been made by an armadillo, a common animal in the area. Now I realized that it was the tortoise's den. Just before he reached the hole, I caught him and picked him up. He hissed grumpily and swung his thick front legs about, trying to get free. He was almost fourteen inches long from the front of his shell to the back. He must have weighed about fifteen pounds. I wondered what to do with him. I did not really mind his eating the lettuce, although I felt it would be nice to save some of it for myself. I worried, though, that if I left him where he was, my neighbor might catch him and turn him into turtle soup! I certainly did not want that to happen, so I carried him some distance into the piney woods. I put him down in front of an old abandoned armadillo burrow. Right away he began digging with his front legs to make the hole wide enough to fit him. The dirt flew, and in a few minutes he was out of

▲ *Fire promotes the growth of grasses and clears the forest floor. Prescribed, controlled fires are a valuable land-management tool.*

sight. He must have decided he liked his new home, because he did not come back to the garden again.

During the months that followed I discovered there were six or seven good-sized gopher tortoises living on my eighty acres. Most of the time they kept to themselves, but now and then I saw one sunning itself at the mouth of its burrow or eating grass nearby. Meanwhile, I worked hard at turning my land into my own private nature reserve. I called it "the Place." One of the things I did was fight fire. In those days, the people in my area allowed their cattle to roam freely in the woods. Every spring, people set fires in the woods that burned up brush and young trees and any leaves and pine needles lying on the ground. This allowed grass to grow that the cows could eat. I believed that fire was a bad thing because it destroyed the food and shelter that wildlife depended on. When a woods fire started up close to my property, I would put it out myself or call the nearby fire tower for help. Over the years, this complete protection from fire made a big difference. The piney forests on the property became deeper and darker. Thickets grew up everywhere. Young hardwood saplings that would have been killed by fire now were able to grow into tall trees crowded close together. Open ground under the trees disappeared altogether.

Then, one day after I had lived at the Place for almost twenty years, I suddenly realized that my gopher tortoises had disappeared. I had not noticed until it was too late. Worried, I began reading whatever I could find about them. It did not take me long to learn that, in protecting the Place from fire, I had made it an unfit place for tortoises to live. My gophers needed fire. They needed those open spaces under the pines where the grasses they ate could grow. They needed sunny openings where they

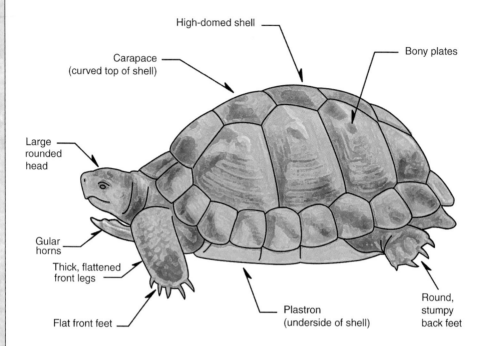

High-domed shell

Carapace
(curved top of shell)

Bony plates

Large
rounded
head

Gular
horns

Thick, flattened
front legs

Flat front feet

Plastron
(underside of shell)

Round,
stumpy
back feet

could dig their burrows, sun themselves, and make nests to lay their eggs in. Woods fires, started by lightning, had been part of the natural scene in this area long before man had moved in. In trying to protect nature without first learning what was the best way to go about it, I had done more harm than good.

I also learned that what had happened on my land was also happening, though often for different reasons, everywhere in the gopher tortoise's range. Gophers had still been fairly common when I bought the Place back in the 1960s. Now, everywhere, the species was on the decline or was gone for good. Sadly, I wondered whether I would ever see these wonderful, ancient creatures on the Place again.

Champion Digger

The family history of tortoises goes back many millions of years. Their earliest known ancestors lived during the Miocene period, marked by evolution of many mammals of relatively modern form.[1] They may have been around even before dinosaurs roamed the earth. The earliest fossils found in North America date from about 55 million years ago. The fossils of twenty-two species of North American tortoises have been found, but only four species survive

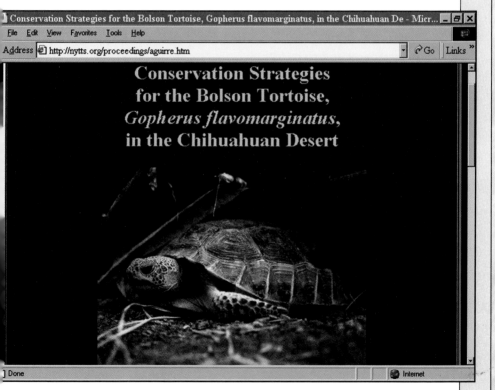

▲ The Bolson, or Mexican, tortoise lives in Mexico.

today. They are the desert tortoise, the Mexican or Bolson tortoise, the Texas or Berlandier's tortoise, and the gopher tortoise.[2] The gopher, Bolson, and desert tortoises are on the United States Fish and Wildlife Service's Endangered Species List. This means that they are in danger of dying off completely, or becoming extinct, so the United States government is trying to protect them.

It is pretty easy to tell tortoises from most other turtles. They are land turtles, for one thing, so they will almost always be found on high, dry ground. Tortoises never bask on logs in ponds and rivers like many turtles do. Unlike some turtles, they are not very colorful. Their heads and legs are grayish black. They have none of the yellow or red markings many water turtles have. Their top shell, called a carapace, is dull brown or blackish brown. Their bottom shell, called a plastron, is yellowish. In adult gopher tortoises, two thick hornlike projections called gular horns stick out at the front of the plastron. Yet probably the best way to recognize a tortoise is to look at its legs. They are very thick and leathery. The back legs are smaller than the front legs. They look like they might belong to a small elephant. Unlike pond turtles, there is no webbing between the back toes. The tortoise's big front legs are flattened, somewhat like a shovel. This is especially true of the gopher tortoise.

▶ A Desert in Disguise

The gopher tortoise is the only one of the four North American tortoises that lives east of the Mississippi River. Its range includes all the Deep South states. In Florida, its range covers most of the state. In the other Southern states it lives only in the coastal plain. The coastal plain includes

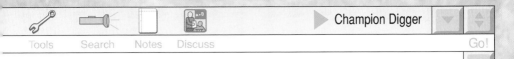

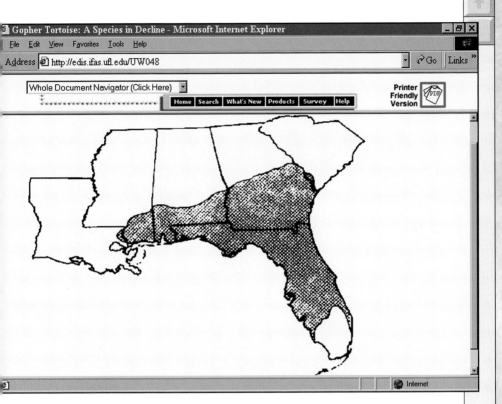

Gopher Tortoise: A Species in Decline - Microsoft Internet Explorer

File   Edit   View   Favorites   Tools   Help

Address http://edis.ifas.ufl.edu/UW048   Go   Links

Whole Document Navigator (Click Here)

Home | Search | What's New | Products | Survey | Help

Printer Friendly Version

Internet

▲ *The gopher tortoise is found only in coastal plains of states like Mississippi, Alabama, Georgia, and Florida. This region is fairly low in elevation and stretches between the Gulf of Mexico and the Atlantic Ocean.*

the areas of those states that are fairly low in elevation and closest to the Gulf of Mexico and the Atlantic Ocean.

The other North American tortoises inhabit dry desert-like country, so you may wonder why the gopher is so at home in the Deep South. After all, the Deep South does not seem much like a desert, with its generous annual rainfall and abundant green vegetation. Yet in some ways the South's coastal plain is a desert in disguise. The soils are sandy and well drained. This means that on and near the surface the soils dry out very quickly, just as in a desert. This is especially true since the weather is very hot

during much of the year. In the coastal plain the soils are not very fertile either. Only plants and trees that are adapted to such soils do well. Unlike a desert, there are forests here. Under natural conditions, though, they are open-looking forests that allow a lot of sunlight to reach the ground. These forests are made up mostly of Southern pine trees, like slash and loblolly, along with some oaks, such as blackjack and turkey oak. However, one pine tree dominated the coastal plain until man changed things: the longleaf pine.

The Need for Fire

The longleaf is a beautiful tree that grows to be 120 feet tall. It is named for its long shiny needles, which can measure up to a foot long. Early settlers wrote of traveling for mile after mile through endless forests of longleaf pines. Compared to many other types of forest, this one was easy to walk in. The trunks of the pines were usually spaced widely apart and rose straight as telephone poles. Sunlight fell on the forest floor, and the ground was mostly open. It was kept that way by woods fires. No area of the country is hit by more lightning bolts than the Southern coastal plain. As a result, fires were common in the old days. There were no roads or firefighters to stop the fires, so a single fire could burn many thousands of acres. Longleafs were adapted to deal with fire. Their thick, fire-resistant bark protected the big trees. Little longleaf seedlings hugged the ground during their first three years, setting down a deep root. Then they would grow quickly, often more than a foot a year. In a few years, they were out of reach of the flames.

Because fires occurred so often, they kept brush and young hardwoods—which are not very fire resistant—from

▲ Nature preserves such as the Kennedy Space Center in Florida use fire management to make a suitable environment for gopher tortoises.

crowding out the native grasses and legumes that grew under the pines. This created just the right habitat for gopher tortoises to live in. Tortoises, with their heavy shells and thick, stumpy legs, are not built to get around easily. They need fairly open ground in which to maneuver. Even more important, they depend on many kinds of grasses and grassy plants called forbs and legumes for food. Forbs are herbs other than grass. An example of a legume used for fodder is clover. Wherever shrubs and thickets take over, these grasses and plants are crowded out, and so are the tortoises that depend on them.

▶ Built-in Shovels

One of the most amazing things about the gopher tortoise is its talent for digging. All tortoises do some digging, but the gopher is, by far, the champion. The Texas tortoise has wrist joints in its front legs that it can bend to some degree. The gopher tortoise's wrist joint, however, is covered by strong ligaments that hold it tightly in place. The result is that the gopher can use its forelegs like shovels. The leg is the handle and the foot is the blade. There is no "give" between them. This makes it possible for a gopher to move a lot of dirt around.

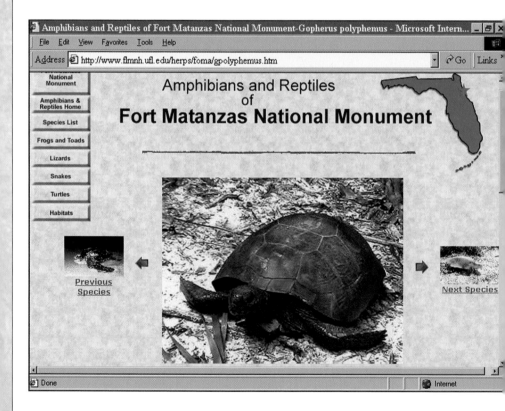

▲ The front legs of a gopher tortoise are very stiff. They work like shovels and are excellent tools for digging.

The gopher uses its digging skills for two purposes: to make nests for its eggs and to make the burrows in which it lives. It always chooses nest and burrow sites that get plenty of sunlight. The burrows are amazing constructions. They can be up to 35 feet long—there is one record of a burrow that was 47 feet long.[3] However, in some places in Mississippi burrows average only about ten feet long. That may be because the earth under the sandy topsoil is composed of hard clay. Even with a real shovel, it would be tough digging holes just three or four feet deep.

▶ A Microhabitat

The gopher digs its burrow by scooping first with one foot, then with the other. It pivots back and forth, throwing a lot of dirt behind it that will later become the entrance mound or "apron." The tunnel slants down at about a 30-degree angle. It is just wide enough to allow the tortoise to turn around at any point along its length. Usually the tunnel is straight, but sometimes it curves around a root or other obstruction. It may go down as deep as ten feet before the tortoise decides that it is long enough. Then, at the bottom, the tortoise digs out a larger space, a sort of small room, where it can sleep comfortably. These rooms, or chambers, are so deep down that they are not affected by changes in the weather. The tortoise creates its own world—what scientists call a microhabitat. It has its own microclimate, where the temperature and humidity hardly change at all, no matter whether it is hot summer or cold winter aboveground.

Sometimes tortoises dig the tunnel so that it turns upward just before the little chamber. That way, if water flows down from the surface, it collects at the bottom of the tunnel rather than in the room where the gopher

sleeps. Tortoises do not seem to mind a good soaking. Scientists have found them submerged in rainwater at the bottom of their burrows for days on end, especially in winter. This makes good sense from a tortoise's point of view. Tortoises eat very little, if anything, during the winter months. Like other animals, they run the risk of losing body moisture when they are fasting. That does not happen as long as they stay wet. Of course, there can be too much of a good thing. Sometimes unhappy-looking gophers will sit at the entrances of burrows that are flooded after heavy thunderstorms. When that happens, the soil usually absorbs the water quickly. Before long the burrow is dry again.

Baby gopher tortoises sometimes live for a while in an adult's burrow. Usually, though, they dig small burrows of their own, or they simply bury themselves in loose sand or piles of dead leaves.

▶ Gophers at Home

Tortoises are not exactly sociable, but they like to live in loose groups, or colonies. In habitat where they are protected,

---

AN OBSERVATION

ONE OF THE GOPHERS ON MY PROPERTY MAINTAINED HOMES ON TWO SAND RIDGES THAT WERE OVER 200 YARDS APART. IN BETWEEN WAS MY HOUSE AND A POND, ENCLOSED BY A FENCE. THE FENCE AND POND CREATED A BARRIER THAT SHE HAD TO GO AROUND. I FIGURED THAT SHE HAD TO TRAVEL ALMOST A QUARTER OF A MILE TO GET FROM ONE BURROW TO THE OTHER. THAT IS A LONG JOURNEY FOR A TORTOISE WEARING A HEAVY SHELL. OF COURSE, ONCE SHE SETTLED INTO ONE OF HER BURROWS, SHE USUALLY STAYED PUT FOR WEEKS OR EVEN MONTHS AT A TIME.

▲ *Gopher tortoises are herbivores. They eat grasses, mushrooms, and berries. In Mississippi, where this tortoise lives, grasses like panicgrass, wiregrass, and bluestem grass make tasty meals.*

where there is plenty of food, and there are good sites for burrows, half a dozen tortoises may share a single acre. During their lifetimes they will dig several burrows. From one season to another, or even from one day to another, they may move back and forth between two or three burrows. When they do this often, the trails they make are easy to see. Usually the burrows are fairly close to each other.

Each gopher tortoise has a home territory that can vary from less than one acre to two or three acres, depending on the food supply. Males usually have larger territories than females. Males also move around more, especially during the spring and early summer breeding season, when they are looking for females.

Gophers are herbivorous; that is, vegetarian. They are not fussy, eating a wide variety of grasses and broad-leaved

plants that grow in sandy soils. However, they have their preferences. Here in Mississippi some of their favorites are panicgrass, wiregrass, and bluestem grass.[4] They also eat mushrooms and berries. Seeds from plants they eat, like dew berries and blackberries, pass right through their digestive system. In this way, gophers "plant" a new crop of the foods they like best in the neighborhood of their burrows. Their grazing keeps the grass low. This "mowing" makes it easier for the seeds they deposit to grow. In a way, you could say that they plant their own gardens.

▶ Tortoise Landlords and Their Tenants

On warm days, gophers often bask in the sun on the aprons of their burrows. They spend most of their time inside, though, so it is not surprising that a lot of their body wastes collect there. This natural fertilizer helps to give special meaning to the word "microhabitat." A whole host of tiny invertebrates, from insects to microscopic bacteria and protozoa, live in the small hothouse chambers created by the tortoise. They are called invertebrates because, unlike "higher" animals, they have no backbone. In each tortoise burrow, these creatures live in a micro-habitat, a small world, that is one-of-a-kind. When a tortoise abandons a burrow, that unique world dies. However, long before that happens, a gopher may decide to do some housecleaning. Scientists have observed them backing out of their burrows, pushing and scraping out dung and other trash that they dump at a distance from the entrance.[5]

Invertebrates are not the only ones that find gopher burrows useful. Gophers are tolerant landlords. The list of creatures that move in with them, full- or part-time, is amazingly long. Foxes, skunks, opossums, weasels,

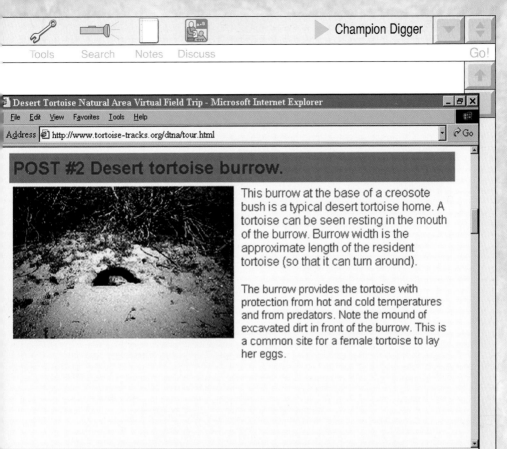

Desert Tortoise Natural Area Virtual Field Trip - Microsoft Internet Explorer

File   Edit   View   Favorites   Tools   Help

Address http://www.tortoise-tracks.org/dtna/tour.html   Go

POST #2 Desert tortoise burrow.

This burrow at the base of a creosote bush is a typical desert tortoise home. A tortoise can be seen resting in the mouth of the burrow. Burrow width is the approximate length of the resident tortoise (so that it can turn around).

The burrow provides the tortoise with protection from hot and cold temperatures and from predators. Note the mound of excavated dirt in front of the burrow. This is a common site for a female tortoise to lay her eggs.

Done   Internet

The Eastern indigo snake seeks shelter in the desert tortoise's burrow during the winter months. A decline in population of the desert tortoise has resulted in a decline in population of the Eastern indigo snake.

burrowing owls, wood rats, several kinds of mice, and even coyotes have all been known to make use of gopher tortoise burrows. When fires sweep through the piney woods, many small creatures like rabbits, mice, lizards, toads, and snakes may escape the flames by hurrying to the safety of a gopher's underground home. It also offers refuge from other threats.

Some animals are so dependent on gopher tortoise dens that, when gophers disappear, they often disappear too—this is why gophers are called a keystone species. Take the Eastern indigo snake for example. This snake

evolved in the same sort of sandy, pine woods habitat as the gopher tortoise. In fact, the range of the indigo snake is almost exactly the same as that of the gopher. Now the species is so rare that the federal government classifies it as threatened wherever it still survives. In Mississippi it seems to have disappeared altogether. There are many reasons why the indigo snake has fallen on hard times, all of them due to humans. However, probably the most important reason is the decline in gopher tortoise populations.[6] The snake needs gopher burrows for refuge and especially for

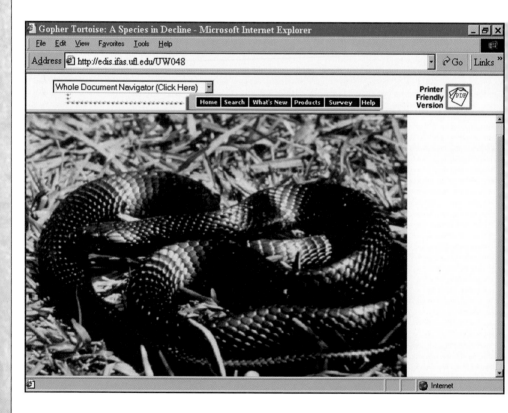

▲ The Eastern indigo snake also resides in gopher tortoise burrows. Unfortunately, with the decline of the gopher, Eastern indigo snakes have lost their homes, and their population is declining as well. They are now a federally listed endangered species.

winter hibernation. One research project in Georgia showed that 94 percent of indigo snakes spent the winter in tortoise burrows. Gophers may still be found in places where there are no indigo snakes, but indigo snakes are not found in places where there are no gophers.

Among other vanishing species that depend heavily on gopher tortoises and their burrows for survival are the black pine snake, the gopher frog, and the Florida mouse. People might wonder why it matters if a certain snake or frog or mouse becomes extinct. After all, there are lots of other kinds of snakes and frogs and mice. Some do not realize that when even one species is lost much more is lost. The fact that some species have such special needs that only the gopher tortoise can supply what they require to survive is evidence of how all species depend on other species to survive. People are no exception.

Chapter 3 ▶

Natural Scheme of Things

The gopher tortoise, of course, does not understand its own importance to other animals. Its simple concern is to keep on living as long as it can and to have offspring so its species will survive. If they are lucky, gophers can live a long time—sixty years or more. However, like most species that have a long life span, they reproduce at a very slow rate. It takes a gopher tortoise about as long as a human to reach an age when it is capable of breeding. Females reach sexual maturity when they are ten or eleven years old at the very earliest. More often, they are between fourteen and

▲ *Gopher tortoises spend most of their time in their burrows. A burrow can be up to 35 feet long.*

twenty years old. On average, males mature a year or two earlier than females.[1]

Usually, tortoise courtship occurs in the spring, but occasionally it has also been observed in the fall. A female will not mate until she is ready. Male tortoises will sometimes parade in front of a female's burrow for hours while she remains just inside the entrance. To keep the male out, she may turn her body sideways to block the tunnel. Sometimes, however, she will allow the male to share the burrow with her, although there is no room for mating to occur there. Even when the female accepts the male's advances, the courtship ritual can last a long time. The male circles the female, stopping often to bob his head vigorously up and down. (Tortoises do not just bob their heads when they are courting. They always seem to do it whenever they are excited.) After the head bobbing and the circling have gone on for a while, the male comes up to the female and nips at her front legs and the gular scutes under her chin. Since females never bite other tortoises, male or female, biologists suspect that this behavior is the male's way of showing that he really is a male.

Although a tortoise's shell is very useful for protection, it is not helpful for mating. In fact, mating is possible only because the mature male tortoise has a concave hollow—a shallow dent—in his plastron. This enables him to fit over the female's curved carapace. Even so, it is a tricky balancing act, and it may take a great many tries before mating finally takes place.

▶ Digging Nests and Laying Eggs

A female gopher tortoise may lay her eggs at any time between early spring and midsummer. Most nesting occurs in May and June. In some study colonies, most of the

females prefer to make their nests right in the apron of dirt at the entrance to their burrows. They may choose this site because it is the sunniest spot around, or perhaps it is easier to dig in the apron soil. In other colonies, however, females dig nests at some distance from the burrow.

Either way, making the nest and laying the eggs is hard work. The female tortoise uses first her hind feet, then her front feet to dig out a depression in the ground. In it she lays a clutch of eggs the size of Ping-Pong balls, letting out long sighs all the while. When she is done, she very

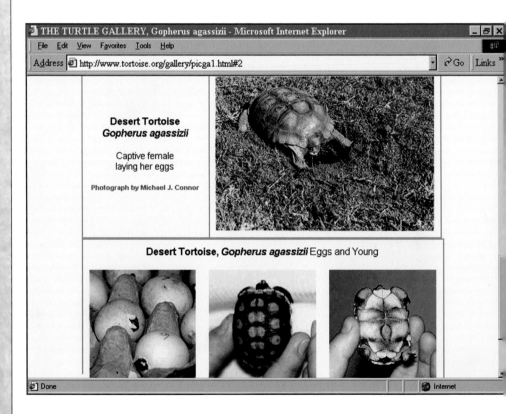

Like the gopher tortoise, the female desert tortoise works hard to make a proper nest. When she has laid her eggs, she camouflages the nest. The eggs are only the size of Ping-Pong balls, and the hatchlings are no bigger than walnuts.

AN OBSERVATION

I HAVE ONLY KNOWN OF TWO NESTS ON MY PLACE IN MISSISSIPPI. ONE WAS IN A BURROW APRON, AND THE OTHER WAS ABOUT THIRTY YARDS AWAY FROM THE NEAREST BURROW. BOTH NESTS GOT A LOT OF SUNLIGHT, BUT THE ONE IN THE APRON WAS SURROUNDED BY THICK GRASS AND BRUSH. THE AREA AROUND THE OTHER NEST WAS VERY OPEN.

---

carefully covers them with dirt, again using her hind feet and then her front feet. When the depression is filled, she uses her front claws to smooth the surface, trying to disguise the nest.

Younger and smaller females may only produce two to four eggs per clutch. The clutches in most of the gopher's range average six to eight eggs, though. Tortoises in central Florida produce much larger clutches than tortoises that live anywhere else—as many as twenty-five eggs—but researchers do not know why.

Many Threats Face Eggs and Hatchlings

Once the mother gopher has buried her eggs, her work is done. The length of time the eggs need to incubate before they hatch seems to depend on where they are laid. In Florida's hot, humid climate, it may only take eighty days. In Georgia, though, it may take more than one hundred days. Wherever it comes into the world, one thing is certain: A baby tortoise has a rough road ahead of it. Raccoons, opossums, gray foxes, and armadillos are among those who relish a meal of gopher eggs. Some biologists think that an introduced species (one that is not native to the Deep South), the imported red fire ant, is an even worse threat. These fierce and unwelcome pests have

AN OBSERVATION

YEARS AGO, I CAME UPON A MOTHER TORTOISE AS SHE WAS DIGGING HER NEST—SOMETHING THAT EVEN SCIENTISTS WHO STUDY GOPHERS RARELY HAVE A CHANCE TO SEE. THIS WAS THE NEST THAT WAS SOME DISTANCE FROM THE MOTHER GOPHER'S BURROW. I WAS VERY EXCITED. I BUILT A WIRE CAGE AND PLACED IT OVER THE NEST TO PROTECT IT FROM PREDATORS. I ALSO SCATTERED A CHEMICAL THAT KILLS FIRE ANTS, AROUND THE SITE. IN SOME PARTS OF ITS RANGE, INCLUDING SOUTHERN MISSISSIPPI, GOPHERS FACE ANOTHER THREAT BEFORE THEY CAN LEAVE THE NEST. IF THE SOIL AT THE NEST SITE IS NOT SANDY ENOUGH, AND ESPECIALLY IF THERE HAS BEEN A DROUGHT, THE HATCHLINGS MAY BECOME "ENTOMBED." THIS MEANS THAT, WHEN THEY BREAK OUT OF THEIR SHELLS, THEY CAN NOT GET TO THE SURFACE BECAUSE THE GROUND IS TOO HARD-PACKED, SO THEIR NEST BECOMES THEIR TOMB.

I HAD EVERY REASON TO BELIEVE THAT, WITH THESE PRECAUTIONS, THE BABIES WOULD HATCH IN SAFETY. YET IT WAS NOT TO BE. THERE WAS A TERRIBLE DROUGHT THAT SUMMER. I WAITED AND WAITED. EIGHTY DAYS. NINETY DAYS. ONE HUNDRED. THE SURFACE OF THE NEST REMAINED UNBROKEN. FINALLY, AFTER CHECKING WITH A BIOLOGIST WHO IS AN AUTHORITY ON GOPHERS, I DUG UP THE NEST. THERE WERE THREE TINY HATCHLINGS, ALL DRIED UP. THEY HAD GOTTEN THEMSELVES FREE OF THEIR SHELLS, BUT THEY HAD NOT BEEN ABLE TO DIG FREE OF THE HARD EARTH. I FELT SAD FOR DAYS, THINKING ABOUT THEIR BAD LUCK. BUT I CONSOLED MYSELF WITH THE THOUGHT THAT THEIR MOTHER WAS STILL ALIVE, AND NEXT YEAR SHE WOULD TRY AGAIN.

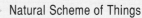

spread throughout the South. They have done terrible harm to many native species of birds, small animals, and reptiles that nest on the ground. The gopher tortoise is one of these. If fire ants find a clutch of its eggs, they will eat them.

Once a tortoise hatchling does get free of the nest, its chances improve with every month that it manages to survive. The first couple of years are the most dangerous. Baby gophers are not much larger than a walnut, and their shells are quite soft. Just about everything that eats meat regards them as a snack, from crows and snakes, to skunks,

Female gopher tortoises cover their clutch of eggs with dirt to protect them from predators. On average, a clutch will contain eight to ten eggs.

raccoons, and fire ants. It is estimated that, on average, about 90 percent of hatchlings do not make it past their second year. After that, however, their shells harden and they are no longer bite-size, so the odds get better.

If they can make it to their eighth or ninth year, their chances of living a long life are very good, since mature tortoises have few natural enemies. According to nature's plan, tortoises can afford to have a low reproductive rate because they have years and years in which to produce enough surviving offspring to replace them when they die.

Chapter 4

A Tortoise's Worst Enemy

During the millions of years that tortoises have lived on earth they have had to deal with many hard times. The great changes in climate that caused dinosaurs to become extinct and allowed warm-blooded animals to evolve had an effect on tortoises too. During the Miocene epoch, dry grassland—ideal for tortoises—stretched all across

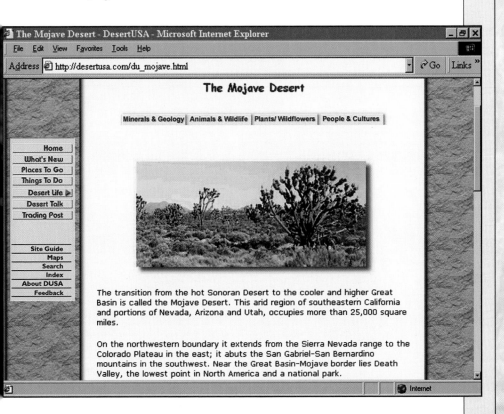

The transition from the hot Sonoran Desert to the cooler and higher Great Basin is called the Mojave Desert. This arid region of southeastern California and portions of Nevada, Arizona and Utah, occupies more than 25,000 square miles.

On the northwestern boundary it extends from the Sierra Nevada range to the Colorado Plateau in the east; it abuts the San Gabriel-San Bernardino mountains in the southwest. Near the Great Basin-Mojave border lies Death Valley, the lowest point in North America and a national park.

▲ The Texas, Bolson, and desert tortoises all live in the warm desert regions such as the Mojave or Sonoran Deserts.

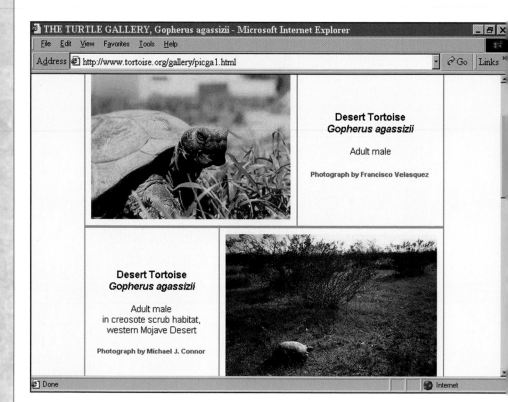

Desert Tortoise
Gopherus agassizii

Adult male

Photograph by Francisco Velasquez

Desert Tortoise
Gopherus agassizii

Adult male
in creosote scrub habitat,
western Mojave Desert

Photograph by Michael J. Connor

▲ *The desert tortoise.*

North America. When the climate changed, much of that grassland disappeared. Three of the four surviving species of North American tortoises, the Texas, the desert, and the Bolson tortoise, held out in warm desert regions of the West. The fourth species, the gopher tortoise, adapted to the climate and soils of the southeastern United States. In these places they have continued to survive and do well for thousands and thousands of years, until now.

Now, these ancient creatures must deal with our species, and they do not know how to do that. As a result, their population is declining in all the regions where they live. In much of their historic range they have completely disappeared.

▶ Humans versus Tortoises

For the gopher, as for the other tortoise species, it has been a sad story. The tortoise has been slaughtered for food ever since humans first inhabited this continent. It is easily caught if it is surprised away from its burrow. If it is inside, people can use a long hook to drag it out, or they can dig a pit at the burrow entrance; when the tortoise tries to leave, it falls in. In spite of this, tortoises managed to fare pretty well in much of their range until the last fifty years or so. Then, it seems as though everything that could go wrong for them did go wrong.

Until very recently, thousands of young gopher tortoises were collected and sold as pets, even though the collectors knew that they almost never survived in captivity.[1] In many parts of the South, gophers have become the unintended victims of rattlesnake roundups. Snake hunters catch lots of rattlesnakes. They handle the snakes and "milk" them of their venom, showing off for the crowds at country fairs. Rattlesnakes often hide in gopher tortoise burrows, and in order to capture them, some hunters pipe gasoline into the burrows. The rattlesnake usually comes out looking very sick. The gopher tortoise usually stays inside and dies from breathing in the fumes.

Another major cause of mortality for tortoises (and for hundreds of other species of wildlife), is the automobile. Thousands of gopher tortoises have been crushed on highways. As more and more highways are built, gophers increasingly have to cross roads to get from one place to another. If they are not killed by a car, they may be picked

D. Rich 12/94

▲ *Gopher tortoises need open, sunny places to live.*

up by its driver and carried off. In captivity, they are often deprived of their natural diet and are not able to dig to their heart's content. They are likely to become ill and deformed, their legs horribly thin and their shells misshapen. Eventually, if they do not die first, the person keeping them may decide to turn them loose.

▶ Doing More Harm Than Good

Releasing a captive tortoise back into its natural environment can be even more harmful than capturing it in the first place. Scientists now suspect that the release of sick captive tortoises may be at least partly responsible for the spread of a terrible disease that is infecting whole colonies of wild tortoises. It is caused by a bacterium called mycoplasma. It has been named Upper Respiratory Tract Disease (URTD) because, like a deadly flu, it interferes with the tortoise's ability to breathe. The tortoise gradually loses appetite, sickens, and dies.

Scientists first found the disease in desert tortoises back in the 1980s.[2] Desert tortoises were already in serious trouble. People were moving into their desert home. Off-road

The Law and The Tortoise - Microsoft Internet Explorer

File   Edit   View   Favorites   Tools   Help

Address http://tortoisegroup.org/thelaw.html   Go   Links

Why Wild Tortoises Should Not Be Removed from the Desert

It is against the law to collect a wild tortoise without a permit. Tortoises often cross roads through undeveloped desert. **They** know where they are going; they are not lost. The Desert Tortoise is a threatened species and take is not allowed without a special permit. Take means harm, harass, pursue, hunt, shoot, wound, kill, trap, capture, or collect.

There is no reason to rescue it by taking it home or far out into the desert. That is against the law! If you were to pick it up to move it to the side of the road to which the tortoise was heading, that, too, is illegal. It may startle the tortoise and cause it to pass all the water in its bladder. This is water that the tortoise has stored to use over many months. When you cause this water to be lost, the tortoise may die of dehydration. Think twice about moving a tortoise from the road. *If you want a tortoise for a pet, call Tortoise Group.*

Done   Internet

▲ *The desert tortoise population has been devastated by URTD. Many animals have caught this deadly disease from captive tortoises that were released into the wild. Today it is against the law to keep or release a desert tortoise without a permit.*

vehicles (ORVs) were killing them by the thousands. Now this very contagious disease has wiped out 70 to 90 percent of some desert tortoise populations. As though that were not enough bad news, URTD has now turned up in gopher tortoise colonies as well. The disease was first found in South Florida gophers. Now, as scientists feared, other populations, as far west as Mississippi, have become infected.

▶ The Worst Threat of All

All of these threats to the gopher tortoise's future are serious. Yet there is one threat that is worse than all the others put together. With every passing day, the gopher loses more and more of the habitat it calls home. Timber companies have cut and cleared millions of acres of the naturally growing pine forests in which gophers do well. In their place they have planted pine plantations where the young trees are crowded close together and are protected from fire. As a result, there are not enough open sunny spots where gophers can dig burrows and find grasses to eat.

Millions of acres of tortoise habitat have been bulldozed away to make room for new housing developments, or subdivisions. Nowadays, the Deep South is called the Sunbelt to attract people to move there. These new southerners always want the same high and dry land for their homes that the tortoise needs for its home.

The Future of the Gopher Tortoise

Things look pretty grim for the gopher tortoise. However, all is not lost. As far back as 1978, a few dedicated biologists became worried about the gopher's future. They founded the Gopher Tortoise Council as a forum where people could learn about research studies and discuss ways

▲ Habitat destruction is one of the main reasons for the population decline of tortoises in North America. In the southern United States developers create housing developments and golf courses where the coastal plains used to lie.

to save the species. The gopher is now protected by state or federal laws. In Florida it is listed as a "species of special concern." Elsewhere in its range it is listed as threatened or endangered.

By themselves, laws do not do much good. They need to be put into action. Happily, some wildlife refuges, military reservations, and national forests in the Deep South have begun using land-management practices—especially prescribed burning—to improve the habitat for tortoises. A good example is the buffer zone around NASA's Kennedy Space Center in central Florida. Burns are regularly scheduled there. The area now protects one of the largest colonies of tortoises in the state.

▶ A Prescription for Recovery

Still, a lot more needs to be done if the species is to survive. More public land must be set aside as tortoise habitat.[1] Timber companies should be encouraged to manage their properties so that tortoises are still able to live there.[2] More counties need to adopt restrictions that prevent developers

---

AN OBSERVATION

ORDINARY PEOPLE CAN HELP TOO. I AM A GOOD EXAMPLE OF THAT. ONCE I REALIZED I WAS INTERFERING WITH THE NATURAL SCHEME OF THINGS BY PROTECTING MY PROPERTY FROM FIRE, I CHANGED MY WAYS. I BEGAN TO DO CONTROLLED BURNS EVERY TWO OR THREE YEARS. SURE ENOUGH, MY EFFORTS PAID OFF. ONE DAY WHEN I WAS OUT WALKING IN THE PINE WOODS, I WAS THRILLED TO FIND A BIG GOPHER TORTOISE TRUDGING ACROSS MY PATH. HE WAS COMING HOME! IT WAS LIKE GETTING A BIRTHDAY PRESENT WHEN IT WAS NOT EVEN MY BIRTHDAY. SINCE THEN, THAT FIRST TORTOISE HAS BEEN JOINED BY AT LEAST FIVE OF HIS FELLOWS.

In Florida, signs such as this one alert drivers that they must brake for gopher tortoises or face a penalty.

from building subdivisions and golf courses that destroy tortoise colonies.[3] Policies like that would not help just gophers. They would also help the many other wild species that need the same kind of habitat to survive.

Anyone can help by supporting organizations that fight to save endangered wildlife. Anyone living in the Deep South can join a state or local conservation group that protects the gopher tortoise's natural habitat. In the West, anyone can join a group that protects the desert tortoise's or the Bolson tortoise's habitat. In some parts of the tortoises' range, people can plant in their yards the kinds of grasses and plants that tortoises like to eat. People

can be warned not to capture wild tortoises or release tortoises that have been kept as pets. If they happen to see any turtle crossing a road, they can stop and carefully carry it off the road in the direction it was headed.

Gopher tortoises are wonderful, peace-loving creatures. They have lived on Earth much longer than humans have. It would be a terrible crime if they should disappear just because we did not care enough to save them.

The Endangered and Threatened Wildlife List

This series is based on the Endangered and Threatened Wildlife list compiled by the U.S. Fish and Wildlife Service (USFWS). Each book explores an endangered or threatened animal, tells why it has become endangered or threatened, and explains the efforts being made to restore the species' population.

The United States Fish and Wildlife Service, in the Department of the Interior, and the National Marine Fisheries Service, in the Department of Commerce, share responsibility for administration of the Endangered Species Act.

In 1973, Congress took the farsighted step of creating the Endangered Species Act, widely regarded as the world's strongest and most effective wildlife conservation law. It set an ambitious goal: to reverse the alarming trend of human-caused extinction that threatened the ecosystems we all share.

The complete list of Endangered and Threatened Wildlife and Plants can be found at
http://endangered.fws.gov/wildlife.html#Species

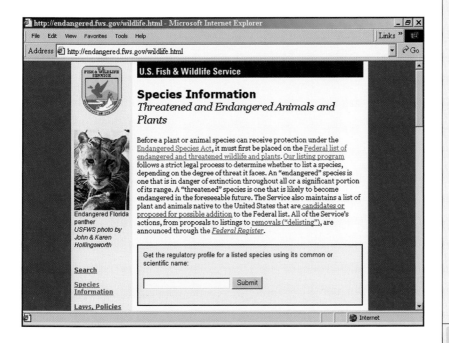

Chapter 2. The Champion Digger

1. Don Stap, "Trials of an Ancient Wanderer," *Audubon*, Jan.-Feb. 1996, vol. 98, no. 1, p. 76.

2. Carl Ernst, Roger W. Barbour, and Jeffrey E. Lovich, *Turtles of the United States and Canada* (Washington, D.C.: Smithsonian Institution Press, 1994), p. 443.

3. Ibid., p. 470.

4. Ibid., p. 476.

5. Ibid., p. 470.

6. *Endangered Species of Mississippi*, Mississippi Department of Wildlife, Fisheries, and Parks, Museum of Natural Sciences, (1992).

Chapter 3. The Natural Scheme of Things

1. Lora L. Smith, "Nesting Ecology, Female Home Range and Activity, and Population Size and Structure of the Gopher Tortoise, *Gopherus Polyphemus*, on the Katherine Ordway Preserve, Putnam County, Florida," Bulletin, Florida Museum of Natural History, 1995, vol. 38, part 1 of 4, p. 97.

Chapter 4. A Tortoise's Worst Enemy

1. Carl Ernst, Roger W. Barbour, and Jeffrey E. Lovich, *Turtles of the United States and Canada* (Washington, D.C.: Smithsonian Institution Press, 1994), p. 477.

2. Grace Sheryl McLaughlin, "Upper Respiratory Tract Disease in Gopher Tortoises, *Gopherus Polyphemus*: Pathology, Immune Responses, Transmission and Implications for Conservation and Management." (Ph.D. dissertation) University of Florida, (1997), p. 6.

Chapter 5. The Future of the Gopher Tortoise

1. *The Gopher Tortoise: A Species in Decline*, (pamphlet) Gopher Tortoise Council, c/o Florida Museum of Natural History, P.O. Box 117800, University of Florida, Gainesville, FL 32611.

2. Contact the Gopher Tortoise Council, c/o Florida Museum of Natural History, P.O. Box 117800, University of Florida, Gainesville, FL 32611.

Further Reading

Baskin-Salzberg, Anita. *Turtles*. Danbury, Conn.: Franklin Watts Inc., 1998.

Burns, Diane L. *Frogs, Toads, & Turtles*. Milwaukee, Wis.: Gareth Stevens Inc., 1999.

Conant, Roger. *Peterson Field Guide to Eastern Reptiles*. Boston: Houghton Mifflin Company, 1998.

Levibiel, Timothy. *Turtles*. Poway, Calif.: Wildlife Education, Limited, 1997.

Papastavrou, Vassili. *Turtles & Tortoises*. Danbury, Conn.: Franklin Watts Inc., 1992.

Paull, Richard Cary. *The Gopher Tortoise and Commensals*. Homestead, Fla.: Green Nature Books, 2001.

——. *Tortoises of Mexico and the United States*. Homestead, Fla.: Green Nature Books, 2001.

Peterson, Roger Tory, ed. *Peterson Field Guide to Western Reptiles and Amphibians*. Boston: Houghton Mifflin Company, 1998

Serventy, Vincent. *Turtle & Tortoise*. Austin, Tex.: Raintree Steck-Vaughn Publishers, 1985.

Van Devender, Thomas R. *The Sonoran Desert Tortoise*. Tucson, Ariz.: University of Arizona Press, 2002.

Walls, Jerry G. *Tortoises*. Broomall, Pa.: Chelsea House Publishers, 1999.